LAUNCH PAD LIBRARY

WORLD OF THE RAINFOREST

ROSIE McCORMICK

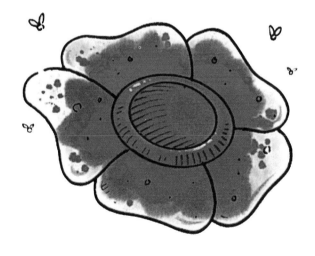

TWO CAN

In association with
FRANKLIN WATTS

How to use this book

Cross references

Above the heading on the page, you will find a list of subjects in the book which are connected to the topic. Look at these pages to find out more about the subjects.

See for yourself

See for yourself bubbles give you the chance to test out some of the ideas in this book. They explain what you will need and what you have to do to see if an idea really works.

Quiz corner

In the quiz corner, you will find a list of questions. The answers to the quiz questions are somewhere on the two pages. Can you answer all the questions about each topic?

Glossary

Difficult words are explained in the glossary near the back of the book. These words are in **bold** on the page. Look them up in the glossary to find out what they mean.

Index

The index is at the back of the book. It is a list of words about everything mentioned in the book, with page numbers next to the words. The list is in the same order as the alphabet. If you want to find out about a subject, look up the word in the index, then turn to the page number given.

Contents

Rainforests of the world

Rainforests are full of thousands of different kinds of trees and flowers. All of the world's rainforests are near the **equator**, which is an imaginary line round the middle of the Earth. Here, it is warm all year and it rains every day. There are rainforests in Africa, South America and Asia.

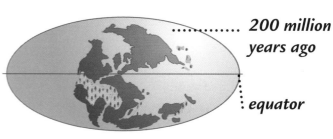

200 million years ago

equator

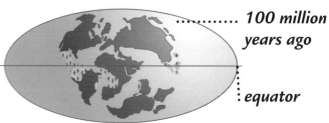

100 million years ago

equator

One land

Millions of years ago, all the land on Earth was joined together in one piece called Pangaea. Animals and plants that lived on Pangaea looked alike. But gradually, Pangaea split into **continents** and slowly the plants and animals in each continent changed to suit their new **environments**.

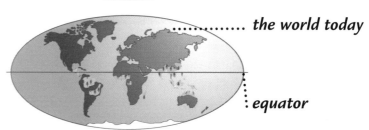

the world today

equator

▲ As Pangaea moved apart, it carried rainforests to different parts of the world.

The top layer of a rainforest is called the canopy.

The middle layer is called the understorey.

The forest floor is dark and hot. Only a little light reaches the floor.

Some trees tower above the canopy. They are called emergents.

Top to toe

Animals live in all parts of a rainforest. Some, such as monkeys, spend their lives high up in the tree branches. Others, such as tigers and peccaries, live on the forest floor.

▼ Most rainforest plants are evergreen, which means their leaves stay green all year round.

Quiz Corner

- In which places do rainforests grow?
- What is the name of the top layer of a rainforest?
- When all the land on Earth was joined together, what was it called?
- What is the middle layer of a rainforest called?

look at: Rainforests of the world, page 4

Weather and water

Rainforest plants play an important part in shaping our weather. They give off water **vapour** which turns into clouds and falls as rain. Rainforest plants soak up the rain and the cycle starts again.

3 When the vapour in the clouds has cooled enough, it turns back into water and falls as rain.

2 The vapour rises into the air. It then starts to cool and forms clouds.

1 The Sun warms the water in oceans, rivers and plants and turns it into vapour.

All the water on our **planet** is **recycled**. It travels from the land and oceans to the air and back again. This movement of water is called the water cycle.

Flooding

Every year, millions of litres of rain falls on rainforests, about half of it into rainforest rivers. The rest falls on to leaves and into the soil. Often, during heavy rains, riverbanks burst and flood parts of the rainforest. Trees help to soak up the water and hold the soil together.

▲ This part of the Amazon rainforest in South America has been flooded by heavy rains.

◀ These rainforest trees in Asia are being cut down and burned to clear the land for farming.

Burning down trees

Each year, rainforest trees are cut down and burned. When trees are burned, they give off a gas called carbon dioxide into the air. Scientists think that if there is too much carbon dioxide in the air it will harm the planet by changing our weather.

Quiz Corner

- What is the movement of water from the land and oceans to the air called?
- What often happens to parts of the rainforest during heavy rains?
- Which gas is given off when trees are burned?

7

look at: Animals of the Amazon, page 10, Rivers and streams, page 20

The Amazon rainforest

The Amazon rainforest in South America is the largest rainforest in the world. It also has the richest plant life, with about 30,000 different kinds of flowers and 4,000 kinds of trees. Like all rainforests, the Amazon has special kinds of plants and animals that do not live anywhere else in the world.

In demand

Mahogany is a **hardwood** tree and takes many years to grow. Every year, lots of mahogany trees are cut down and sent all over the world to be made into furniture. People are worried that soon there will not be any mahogany trees left. They want to protect these trees by making furniture out of trees that grow more quickly.

▲ The Amazon rainforest in South America stretches for thousands of kilometres and crosses into several countries, including Brazil and Peru.

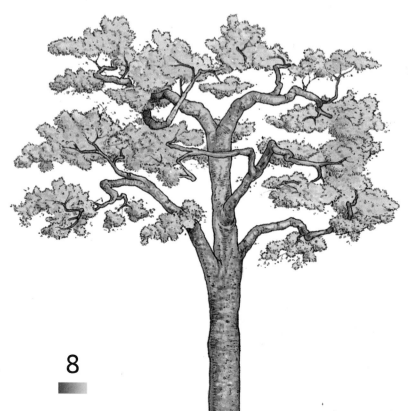

◄ Mahogany trees have long trunks, which can grow up to 25m tall before the first branches appear.

The tree of life

The buriti is a palm tree that is important to local people. It can be made into oil, wine, timber, cork and fertilizer, which farmers use to help their **crops** grow. The buriti grows up to 24m high, which is as tall as a four-storey building.

▼ When it rains, plants called bromeliads fill up with water and small animals, such as frogs, come to live in them.

SEE FOR YOURSELF

See for yourself, by using a fish tank, how plants grow in a hot, wet place. Place a layer of charcoal and gravel at the bottom of the tank and cover with compost. Water the compost and plant ferns and palms. Put a clear cover on top of the tank. Place in the sun and water occasionally.

Growing on trees

Bromeliads grow all over the Amazon rainforest. They wrap their roots around tree branches to keep themselves in place.

Quiz Corner

● In which rainforest plants can frogs live?

● Why is the buriti tree important to local people?

● Name a tree which is sometimes cut down and made into furniture.

9

look at: The Amazon rainforest, page 8, Rivers and streams, page 20

Animals of the Amazon

The Amazon rainforest is a noisy place. From the tallest tree to the forest floor, you can hear birds squawking and monkeys howling. There are animals everywhere, including butterflies, beetles and ants. Hundreds of different kinds of **reptiles** and **amphibians** live in the forest too.

The forest floor
The Amazon forest floor is dark and damp. Few plants grow here because the thick canopy overhead blocks out sunlight which they need to grow. But lots of animals live on the forest floor, including jaguars, agoutis and peccaries.

A jaguar has a patterned coat which helps it to hide among the trees.

Young jaguars learn to defend themselves by playing and fighting with one another.

Many rainforest frogs have colourful poisonous skins to stop other animals from eating them.

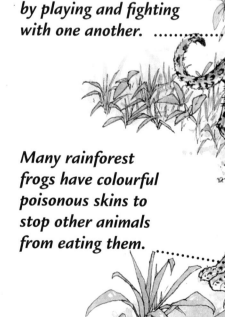

A peccary has strong jaws and sharp teeth. It sniffs around the forest floor, looking for roots, nuts and seeds to eat.

Howler monkeys are some of the noisiest animals that live in the Amazon rainforest. The calls they make to each other in the morning can be heard from far away.

Rainforest birds
More kinds of birds live in the Amazon rainforest than in any other place on Earth. Most live in the canopy.

An agouti lives alone in the forest. It feeds on grass, fruit and roots.

▲ A toucan has an enormous beak, which it uses to pick fruit and insects from the trees.

A chameleon is a reptile. Its feet have long toes which can grip on to tree branches.

Quiz Corner

- Why do few plants grow on the rainforest floor?
- Which animal has a patterned coat to help it hide among the trees?
- What does an agouti feed on?

11

look at: Asian animals, page 14

Asian rainforests

Rainforests stretch across Asia and parts of northern Australia. These rainforests are different from the Amazon rainforest because they do not have such a thick canopy. This means more light reaches the forest floor and many more plants can grow, including trees, flowers and fruits.

▲ Rubber is collected from a rubber tree by stripping off part of the tree's bark. The runny rubber flows into a pot.

Rubber trees

Rubber trees grow in Asian rainforests. The rubber is collected from the trees and used to make tyres, shoe soles and many other things. In the past, rubber trees grew only in South America, but travellers planted young trees in Asia. Today, more rubber trees grow in Asia than anywhere else in the world.

▲ Pitcher plants often grow on the rainforest floor. They feed on insects which crawl into the tube-shaped leaves at the bottom of the plant.

SEE FOR YOURSELF

Make a wall chart. On your chart, draw as many things as you can that are made of rubber or have rubber parts.

Fruits of the forest

Asian rainforests are full of different kinds of juicy fruits, such as mangoes, starfruits and lychees. These fruits are picked when they are nearly ripe and sent all over the world. You may have seen some of them in your local supermarket.

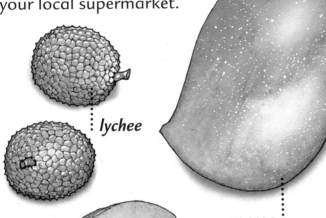

lychee

mango

starfruit

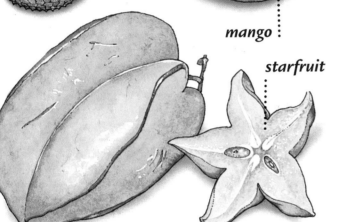

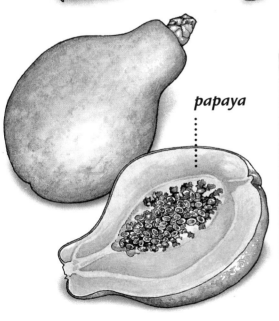

papaya

Plants for weaving

Rattan is a tough and stringy rainforest plant. Long stems of rattan are used to make mats, hats and chairs.

Quiz Corner

● How is rubber collected from a rubber tree?

● What is the name of the largest and smelliest flower in the world?

● What things can you make from rattan?

look at: Asian rainforests, page 12

Asian animals

An Asian rainforest, just like the Amazon rainforest, is home to many different kinds of animals. Thousands of insects crawl over dead leaves and tree branches. Some of these insects are so tiny that you cannot see them, but others are bigger than an adult's hand. Apes, such as orang-utans and gibbons, swing through the canopy, while elephants and tigers roam the forest floor.

CHATTERBOX

Asian elephants live in groups, called herds. Each herd can travel over an area up to 2,000sq km. That's about the same size as a large city.

◀ In Asia, elephants are trained to move heavy logs. They help clear the land for farming.

A tiger is the biggest kind of cat in the world. It hunts alone, travelling long distances every night looking for meat to eat.

Knocking down trees
In India and Southeast Asia, Asian elephants live on the edges of the rainforests. They have small ears and short tusks. Asian elephants eat leaves, which they pick from the trees with their trunks. When the leaves are too high, the elephants knock over the trees to reach them.

14

Quiz Corner

- Do Asian elephants have short or long tusks?
- When do tigers hunt?
- Which kind of eagle lives only on a group of islands in Southeast Asia?

The monkey-eating eagle lives only in the Philippines, which is a group of islands in Southeast Asia. It builds its nest in tall trees that poke above the rainforest canopy.

This snake, called a cobra, is brown to help it blend in with the leaves on the forest floor. This is called **camouflage**.

An orang-utan spends most of its time in the canopy eating fruit, leaves and plants.

The world's largest stick insect is called the Malaysian wood nymph. It is difficult to spot on the forest floor.

look at: African animals, page 18

African rainforests

Some rainforests grow on the sides of mountains. These rainforests are called cloud forests because clouds often cover the tops of the trees and make them look misty. There are cloud forests scattered across Africa.

Mosses and lichens

In African rainforests, thousands of tiny bright green plants, called mosses, grow just beneath the canopy. They cover tree trunks and roots like a soft carpet. Many animals, such as tiny spiders and mites, live in the mosses. Long plants, called lichens, also grow on trees. They hang from the branches and look like cobwebs.

▲ These fungi are growing on the fallen trunk of a rainforest tree.

◄ Mosses and lichens can cover tree trunks and branches, rocks and stones.

Fungus

A fungus does not have leaves or roots and is not green like a plant. It lives on plants and soaks up food from them. Mushrooms and toadstools are kinds of fungi. Many fungi grow well on or near the rainforest floor, where it is damp and dark.

Quiz Corner

- What are mountain rainforests sometimes called?
- Which bright green plants cover tree trunks like a carpet?
- Which animal eats a type of poisonous bamboo?

Bamboo

Bamboo is a grass that grows in warm wet places. It is found on the slopes of many African rainforests. Bamboo flowers only once every 30 years. Animals, such as lemurs, eat its stems, leaves and shoots.

▶ The golden bamboo lemur feeds on a type of bamboo that is poisonous to humans and many other animals.

look at: African rainforests, page 16

African animals

In Africa, many rainforests have been cut down, but a few are left in western Africa. The largest of these stretches across the Democratic Republic of the Congo. Here, animals such as gorillas and chimpanzees live in the trees and on the forest floor.

All together
Gorillas belong to a group of animals called apes. They live together in families, made up of one adult male, several females and their young. Male gorillas are larger than female gorillas. They have shiny grey fur on their backs and are called silverbacks.

Building a nest
Every night, gorillas build nests where they sleep. They break off branches and make a simple platform either in the trees or on the ground.

Bedtime
Gorillas spend their days on the forest floor, eating, playing and cleaning each other. They make their nests just before dark. Each adult gorilla builds its own nest. Baby gorillas sleep with their mother.

▼ Gorillas are vegetarians. They roam the forest floor looking for juicy plant stems, leaves and shoots to eat.

Clever chimpanzees

Chimpanzees also belong to the ape family. Chimpanzees are clever animals and have learned how to make and use simple tools. Unlike gorillas, chimpanzees eat meat as well as plants.

▲ Chimpanzees are good at climbing and often rest in trees.

Quiz Corner

- In which country would you find Africa's largest rainforest?
- Where do gorillas sleep?
- Which animals have learned to use simple tools?

look at: Weather and water, page 6, The Amazon rainforest, page 8

Rivers and streams

Rivers and streams run through every rainforest. The Amazon River in South America runs through the Amazon rainforest. In some places the river is narrow, but in others it is so wide you cannot see the other side.

Flooding the rainforest
Each year, during the rainy season, the Amazon River bursts its banks and floods parts of the rainforest. When this happens, many plants on the shore are covered by water for up to six months of the year.

▲ The Amazon River splits into hundreds of smaller rivers which twist and wind their way through the rainforest.

A South American river dolphin swims along the Amazon River looking for fish to eat. It has more than 100 sharp teeth in its mouth.

A manatee is the largest animal in the Amazon River. It uses its split top lip to pull up plants from the riverbed to eat.

When the Amazon rainforest is flooded, the water can be very deep. If you wanted to see the forest floor, you would need diving equipment!

Quiz Corner

● Which is the largest animal in the Amazon River?

● Which meat-eating fish swim together in large groups?

● How many teeth does a South American river dolphin have?

A caiman belongs to the same family of animals as alligators. It floats in the water, waiting for prey which it snaps up in its strong jaws.

Piranhas swim together in large groups. They are meat-eating fish and can tear flesh from the bones of their **prey** *in minutes.*

look at: Animals of the Amazon, page 10, Asian animals, page 14

Rainforests at night

Rainforests are just as noisy at night as they are in the day. Some animals sleep, but many others wake up. Animals that come out at night are called **nocturnal**. They live in all parts of the rainforest. Many nocturnal animals have large eyes, big ears and a good sense of taste and smell. This helps them to find food easily in the dark.

The night monkey is the only nocturnal monkey in South America. It lives in the Amazon rainforest.

Night eyes
Most nocturnal animals can see well in the dark. This is because they have large eyes which take in more light than small eyes. Often, the eyes of nocturnal animals seem to glow in the dark.

An African bushbaby eats sugary gum found under the bark of some trees. It leaps from tree to tree, using its legs and tail to balance.

Bats

During the day, rainforest bats sleep together in large groups. They hang upside down from trees with their wings folded across their bodies. At night, the bats wake up to feed. They eat insects, fruit and the sweet juice, or nectar, from flowers.

The world's biggest bat is the Malay fruit bat from Southeast Asia. When its wings are open, it is as wide as a big toy kite.

A tarsier has huge saucer-shaped eyes. It lives only in a few rainforests in Southeast Asia. A tarsier uses its long toes with flattened ends to cling to tree branches.

◀ Many nocturnal animals feed on rainforest fruits and flowers. They are attracted by the strong smell of rainforest flowers.

Quiz Corner

- Which name is given to animals that come out at night?
- Where does the largest bat in the world live?
- Why do many nocturnal animals have large eyes?

look at: The Amazon rainforest, page 8

Rainforest peoples

Thousands of **peoples** live in rainforests around the world. Here, they can find all they need. There are plants and fruits to eat and animals to hunt. Some peoples grow **crops**, and many know how to use plants to make medicines.

The Yanomami

The Yanomami are the largest group of peoples living in the South American rainforests. Each morning, Yanomami men go hunting with bows and arrows tipped with poison. Often this poison comes from the skin of a rainforest frog. Boys are allowed to hunt with the men from the age of five but Yanomami women stay at home.

All together

All the Yanomami in a village live in one large, round house called a yano. A yano is made from trees bent into a dome shape and then covered with leaves.

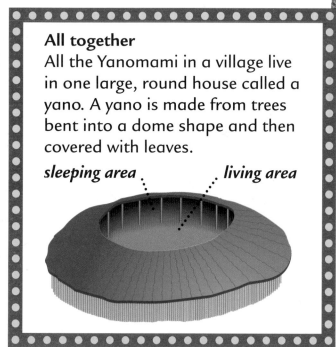

sleeping area   *living area*

▲ Yanomami men hunt monkeys and other animals with bows and arrows.

New neighbours

In the past, only a few peoples lived in rainforests. But in the last 200 years, many more have made their homes here. All these peoples depend on the rainforest for food and shelter.

▲ This Yanomami child's body is decorated with sticks and bead necklaces.

Quiz Corner

- In which rainforests do the Yanomami people live?

- What is the name of the large house where Yanomami people live?

- Where do the Yanomami find the poison for their arrows?

look at: Rainforest peoples, page 24

Forest fruits

Rainforests are one of the richest **resources** on Earth. Some rainforest plants are used to make medicines and others are made into foods, such as oil and fruit juice, or eaten just as they are. Each year, hundreds of new plants are discovered, and many of these are useful too.

Going shopping
Supermarkets all over the world sell hundreds of things from rainforests. Coffee, cocoa, pepper, nuts, bananas, pineapples and avocados all grow in hot, steamy rainforests.

CHATTERBOX

Next time you chew a piece of gum, think about what it is made from. Chicle, which comes from sapodilla trees in the Amazon rainforest, is needed to make chewing gum.

Cape gooseberries are the fruit of a small plant which grows in South America.

Starfruit grow in Asia.

Ginger is a root which grows in Southeast Asia.

Avocados grow in South America.

Brazil nuts grow on tall trees in South America.

Chocolate is made from cocoa beans which grow in South America.

Vanilla is the seed pod of a South American orchid.

Coffee beans grow in Africa and South America.

Some cosmetics are made from rainforest oils and fruits.

Pineapples are a valuable rainforest fruit.

Cola is made from the kola nut which grows in Africa.

*Bananas are an important food **crop**.*

Life savers

Different parts of plants are used to make medicines to treat illnesses, such as heart disease and cancer. The rosy periwinkle plant from Madagascar is used to make a medicine which helps to fight a type of cancer, called leukaemia.

Papaya is a sweet fruit.

Peanuts grow in South America and Africa.

Lychees are the fruits of an Asian tree.

Nutmeg is a spice used to flavour food.

Cinnamon is the dried bark of a Southeast Asian tree.

Cashew nuts grow in Asia and South America.

Pepper is one of the earliest known spices.

SEE FOR YOURSELF

Make a 'forest fruits' scrapbook. Collect pictures of rainforest plants, flowers and fruits. Divide your scrapbook into sections for the different rainforests in the world. Stick each picture in the correct section and label it.

Quiz Corner

● Can you name six things that grow in the rainforests?

● What is chicle used for?

● Which country does the rosy periwinkle plant come from?

look at: Rainforests of the world, page 4

Saving the forests

Huge areas of rainforest have been cut down for timber and to clear land for farming. Trees have also been cut down so that gold and silver can be mined, or dug out of the ground. If we carry on destroying rainforests, they could disappear completely, along with all the plants and animals that live in them.

▶ Today, furniture is often made from **softwood** trees, such as pine.

▲ These enormous trees come from the Amazon rainforest in South America. Workers use electric saws to cut timber, which is sold all around the world.

Wood for furniture
People make furniture from softwood, which grows quickly, rather than from slow-growing **hardwood**. This helps to make sure there will always be enough trees. In many rainforests, when trees are cut down, new ones are planted.

Keeping rainforests safe
Some rainforests have been turned into national parks. Here, it is against the law to cut down trees. National parks help to keep all the animals, plants and people that live in the rainforests safe from harm.

▲ These people in Southeast Asia are planting young eucalyptus trees. Most of the rainforest around them has already been burned down.

Keeping an eye on things

Around the world, special **conservation** groups, including the Worldwide Fund for Nature, work hard trying to save rainforests. They tell everyone what is happening to the people, plants and wild animals that live in the rainforests. Find out from your local group what you can do to help.

Quiz Corner

● Why have huge areas of rainforest been cut down?

● Why have some rainforests been turned into national parks?

● How can replanting trees help to protect the rainforest?

Amazing facts

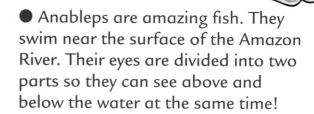

☆ Did you know that the leaves of different rainforest trees never touch or overlap, even though they grow close together. This means that all the leaves get as much sunlight as possible.

● Marmosets live in the Amazon rainforest. They are the only monkeys to drink tree juices. They use their special teeth to cut through the tree bark and suck out the liquid.

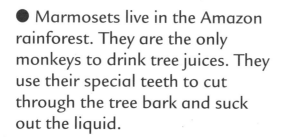

☆ Thornbugs are insects that live in South American rainforests. They sit mostly on thorny tree branches, sucking out juices from under the bark. Thornbugs look like thorns, which stops other animals from eating them.

● Some rainforest plants have enormous leaves. The Victoria water lily of the Amazon River has leaves up to 2m across. They are strong enough for a child to stand on.

● Anableps are amazing fish. They swim near the surface of the Amazon River. Their eyes are divided into two parts so they can see above and below the water at the same time!

☆ Hoatzins are birds that cannot fly well. They live in trees around rivers in South American rainforests. Hoatzin chicks escape from their enemies by jumping from the trees into the rivers. When it is safe, they use claws on their wings and feet to climb back up the trees.

● Sloths are hairy animals that live in South American rainforests. They spend up to 18 hours a day hanging from tree branches without moving.

☆ The world's smallest bat is found in the rainforests of Thailand, in Southeast Asia. It is called the Kitti's hog-nosed bat and is only about 3.5cm long. That's about the size of a large bumblebee!

Glossary

amphibian One of a group of animals, such as frogs, that can live both on land and in the water.

camouflage The markings or colours on an animal which help it to fit in with its surroundings so that it can't easily be seen.

conservation Protecting the planet by looking after the plants and animals that live there.

continent One of the seven big land areas of the world. The continents are Antarctica, North America, South America, Africa, Asia, Europe and Australia.

crops Plants that are grown for food, including wheat, corn and rice.

equator An imaginary line round the centre of the Earth, between the north and south poles.

environment The world around us.

hardwood The wood of trees, such as mahogany. Hardwood trees take many years to grow.

nocturnal Animals that are active at night.

peoples The different groups of people that live in a country.

planet An object in space moving around the Sun or another star.

prey The creatures that another animal hunts and eats.

recycle To use an object or a material again.

reptile One of a group of cold-blooded animals with a skeleton, such as snakes or lizards. A reptile's skin is usually covered with hard scales.

resource A useful or valuable natural thing, such as trees.

softwood The wood of trees, such as rubber and pine. Softwood trees grow more quickly than hardwood trees.

vapour Moisture in the air that can sometimes be seen as steam, mist or clouds.

Index

Created by:
Two-Can Publishing Ltd
346 Old Street
London EC1V 9NQ
and Eljay Yildirim of Thunderbolt,
London

Text: Rosie McCormick
Consultant: Cecelia Fitsimons
Watercolour artwork: Stuart Trotter
and Bill Donohoe
Computer artwork: D Oliver and
Mel Pickering

This edition published 1997 by:
Two-Can Publishing
in association with
Franklin Watts
96 Leonard Street
London
EC2A 4RH

Hardback ISBN 1-85434-409-9
Dewey Decimal Classification 574.5

2 4 6 8 10 9 7 5 3

A catalogue record for this book is
available from the British Library.

Printed and bound in Spain by
Graficromo S.A.

Photographic credits: Biofotos (Brian
Rogers) p12l; Britstock-IFA (Bernd
Ducke) p8; Bruce Coleman p5, p7tr,
p7cl, p11, p29; Colorific! (T Aramac/
Camara Tres) p28; Steve Gorton p26,
p27, p28; Frank Lane Picture Library
(Phil Ward) p18-19c; NHPA (Nigel J
Dennis) p19r; Oxford Scientific Films
(Konrad Wothe) p17r; Premaphotos
(Ken Preston - Mafham) p16-17c;
South American Pictures (Tony
Morrison) p20; Still Pictures (Mark
Edwards) p25; Tony Stone Images
FC; Zefa Pictures p12r, p14, p24.